Business Information Server, BIS
THE Killer App
World"Greatest Productivity APP.
Real-Time Report Processing

Evolutionary Protocycling

Database Power Tools	Web Power Tools	API Power Tools	Admin. Power Tools

➤ **Security ~ Measurement ~ Tracking**

Database	Interactive Processing	Logic Design	Production Use
Form & Report Generators	150 + Macro Logic Functions	Logic & Screen Generators	Logging Monitors History

Users evolve applications to ideal use

Business Information Server, BIS
THE Killer App

A REAL-TIME REPORT PROCESSING SYSTEM
User Designed Applications

After 50+ Years of Development and Improvement; 150+ User Executable Information Power Tools in One System Progression From PC to Mainframe Computers

The Unisys BIS System
By: Louis Schlueter

Real-Time Information Processing

The Unisys Business Information Server
BIS (aka MAPPER);
<u>THE Killer App</u>
<u>And Best Kept IT Secret</u>

The ideal application development system
for new, start up businesses. End users
design reporting applications for each need
that are upward compatible from Windows
Server PC to mid and mainframe system
capabilities as operational growth develops.
IT needs are perfectly matched to evolving
business requirements with
user designed applications.
<u>BIS is a powerful productivity APP</u>
<u>for users on all systems.</u>

Table of Contents

REAL-TIME REPORT PROCESSING
1st Application Design Language
for Users Defined.
BIS Introductory Video

Business Information Server, BIS
THE Killer App
World"Greatest Productivity APP.
Real-Time Report Processing

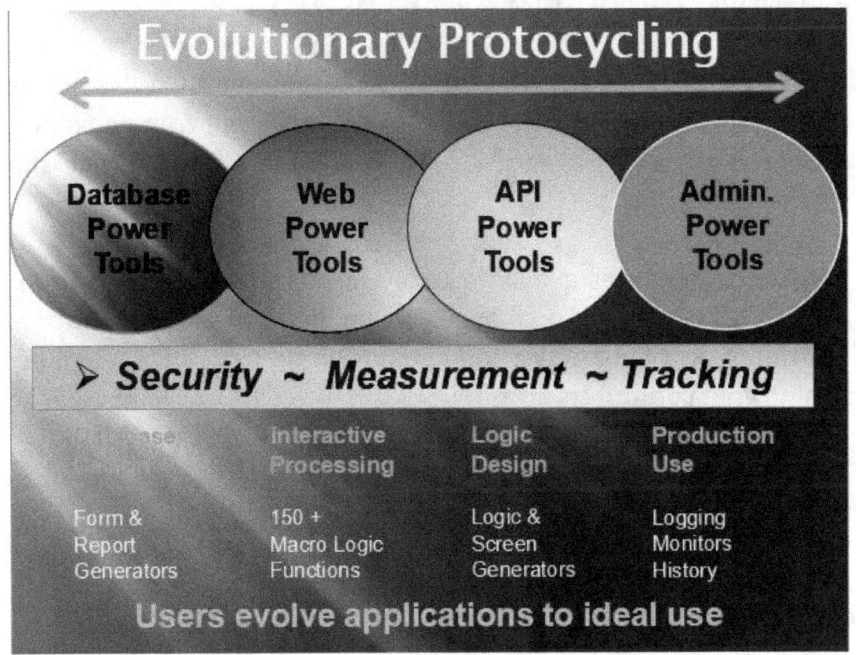

Real-Time Report Processing
The Unisys Business Information Server BIS
(aka MAPPER);
The World's Greatest Productivity
Killer APP
<u>And Best Kept IT Secret</u>

The BIS information processing system is more powerful and has greater general productivity potential than any software systems existing today.   It has all the functionality and productivity producing potential of current software providing WORD PROCESSING, SPREAD SHEETS, GRAPHICS, EMAIL, INSTANT-MESSAGING, SEARCHING, MULT-LEVEL SORTING, EXTENSIVE CALCULATION, REAL-TME DATA BASE UPDATING AND SHARING, FULL SECURITY USER AND DATA BASE MANAGEMENT AND INTERNET ACCESS.   A full set of Coordination (Administrative) tools are available to manage and secure a dynamic, creative user Real-Time Report Processing environment.

All this capability is available today in one Business Information Server (BIS) system and available in hardware configurations providing upward application compatibility from PC's to Mid or Mainframe computers .

It is very likely you have never heard of this system and know nothing of its capabilities Though it was responsible for the sale of >$3 Billion of system sales in Manufacuring, Transportation, Distribution, Retailing, Banking, Insurance, Construction, Energy Production, Recreation, Federal State and City Governments and all the Military Branches.

The story of its creation and evolution to "The World's Greatest Productivity APP and Real-Time Application Development Language for USERS is unique in the computer industry.

It offers enormous productivity potential by its unique, extensive functionality that supports Real-Time Report Processing and the ability of users to design their own data bases and applications without conventional programming.
     This is a 1st[h] Application Development Language for USERS.

Since1968, <u>Added analytic functional additions have been made almost every year since then, hence its functional richness, which is unequaled in the industry.</u> BIS is the World's most powerful productivity APP. THE Killer APP.

User designed, Real-time Report Processing applications have enormous productivity potential and are applicable in the operation of all businesses and institutions from the smallest to the largest. Such productivity and upward compatibility across systems provide enormous tactical and competitive advantages for for BIS users.

There is a trend toward user-oriented computer systems, placing in the hands of the users the ability to direct computer power in application development. BIS is a giant step forward improving productivity with computer technology.

The Business Information Server, BIS Real-Time Report Processing systems, the subject of this book, make accessible to users powerful levels of productivity improvement that are impossible with conventional, structured, professional programming. The BIS system that provides Real-Time Report Processing capabilities, offers in <u>one integrated, hardware scalable software system, the World's Greatest, most powerful productivity APP</u>: THE Killer APP.

BIS Systems can operate across a wide range
of IndustryOpen systems
A user set of over 150 Information Power Tools
(Functions) with over 700 options interactively
executable without programming.
A true, real-time Report Structured Database with
interfaces to industry standard applications and data bases.
A complete, Powerful End User Application
Development Language with Internet accessibility.
Client-Server Networking across a range of
system sizes and vendors.

A full set of system, user management and database
security controls.
Upward application expansion and compatibility from
MS Windows Server PC's to client-server and
individual or interconnected mainframe systems.

**It is greater in productivity potential for all businesses and
institutions than applications such as PC search engines, word
processing and spread sheets combined.**

Tracy Kidder's Pulitzer winning, best selling book "The Soul of a
New Machine described the design and creation of a new computer
system for General Dynamics Corp. In 1981. This describes a
event with <u>much greater IT potential</u>.

BIS offers the 1st Application Design Language for users. Its 50
year history precedes Microsoft PC-DOS and parallels that of its
parent corporation named from Univac to Remington Rand Univac,
to Sperry Univac, to Sperry to its current name of Unisys
Corporation (the merger of Sperry and Burroughs Corporations).
It sold over $3 Billion in systems for Sperry Corporation.

Chapter 1
The Best Kept IT Secret System

**The BIS information processing system is more powerful and
has greater general productivity potential than any software
systems existing today. It has all the analytic functionality and
productivity producing potential of current software providing
WORD PROCESSING, SPREAD SHEETS, GRAPHICS,
EMAIL, INSTANT-MESSAGING, SEARCHING, MULT-
LEVEL SORTING, EXTENSIVE CALCULATION, REAL-
TME DATA BASE UPDATING, FULL SECURITY USER
AND DATA BASE MANAGEMENT AND INTERNET
ACCESS. A full set of Coordination (Administrative) tools are
available to manage and secure a dynamic, creative user Real-
Time Report Processing environment.**

All this capability is available today in one Business Information Server (BIS) system and available in hardware configurations providing upward application compatibility from PC's to Mid or Mainframe computers .

It is very likely you have never heard of this system and know nothing of its capabilities. The story of its creation and evolution to "The World's Greatest Productivity APP is unique in the computer industry.

It offers enormous productivity potential by its unique, extensive functionality that supports Real-Time Report Processing and the ability of users to design their own data bases and applications without conventional programming.

Chapter 2
The Genesis of Real-Time Report Processing

The environment that led to the invention of the concepts and the creation of Real-Time Report Processing software was created in spite of and in opposition to the official policies of the parent corporation, Univac. The year was 1968. It all began in the Sperry Univac Manufacturing Plant in Roseville, Minnesota

Chapter 3

The 418 Report Processing System

Univac had established two main lines of computers; the 1100 line of main-frame computers and a 418 mid-frame line of communications processors.

Univac had recently obtained major contracts to provide United and Eastern Airlines with computer systems to manage their reservation processing. Besides providing the control processors and networks, these contracts also required the first large-scale use of display terminals. These were Uniscope 300 CRT terminals.

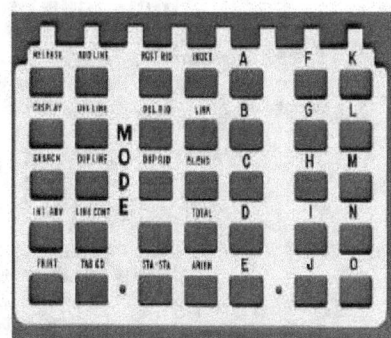

These are dumb terminals with processing done in central processors.

In Feb. 1968, a document entitled "418 Report Processing System" defined the concepts of general purpose Real-Time Report Processing and the system methods for implementing such capabilities. It described the 418 system hardware and software requirements:

Most importantly, the document described the concepts of general purpose Real-Time Report Processing which enabled users to establish reporting applications and process them **without having to program each application. The key was that the user's data became the command language to control Report Processing.**

EXAMPLE: Function command parameters in an Automobile Inventory Database:

```
    ENTER options:          AUTOMOBILE INVENTORY
 *    Make    . Model .  Number .  Price .                        .
 *Automobile .          . License .Wholsale. Retail  . Schedl . 1 .
 *-----------.-------.---------.--------.---------.--------.----
 ********** ******* ********* ******** ********* ******* ***
  BUICK   <Search for a single identity
  BUICK       CENTURY <[AND condition, search for 2 identities]
                    MLS5933 <[OR  search for 2 identities
                    MKL4371 < in same field]
              5,000 <[Search in range, lower value
           R 15,000 <Search in range, upper value]
              +          + <[Verticalsummation/subtotal]
        [Days difference between dates]> +        -
           Sort in alphabetic order]> 1
```

Etc. Full logical computational capabilities are possible. Any number of fields or combinations of Parameters and options can be used. The point is that data and intuitively obvious command parameters are submitted in the context of the user's own data. Reports can be formed as above or they can contain textual or graphic information or any combination of these.

This is why users find Real-Time Report Processing so easy to understand and use. Their own data becomes the command language for Report Processing.

418 CRT Report Processing

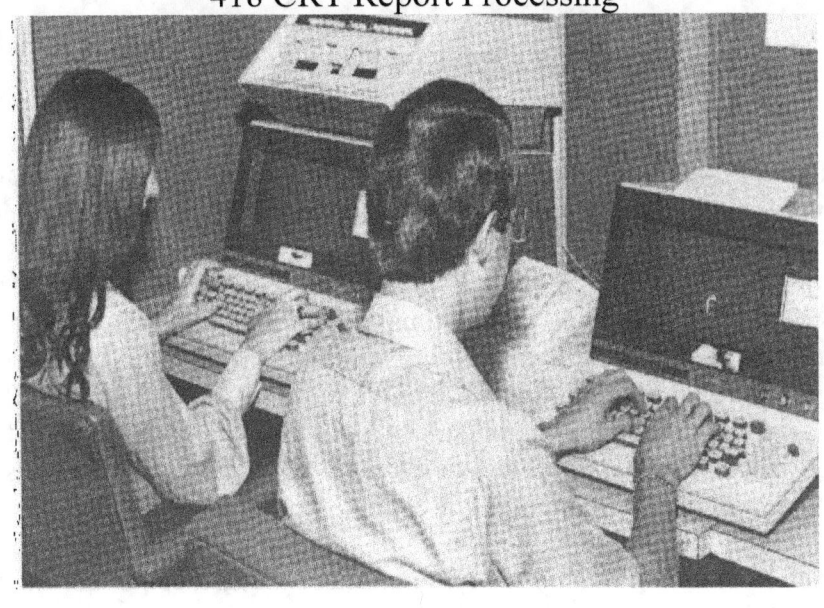

Real-Time Report Processing in Production Control

Chapter 4

The 418 CRT-RPS Growing Pains

This chapter describes some of the lessons learned in having to create these new Report Processing capabilities in a true, real-time environment.

As the service expanded ultimately serving as many as 60 terminals on the 418 processor, the system experienced many growing pains. Also, the developers were learning the nature of Real-Time Report Processing and inventing new techniques to provide new capabilities and to maintain adequate system response time when high volume, concurrent use occurred.

New versions of 418 CRT-RPS system software containing new capabilities were constantly being introduced in the system on a nearly daily basis. These included fixes to software bugs that would only show up under concurrent, multi-user use. Such bugs would usually cause a system crash. Back up and recovery software was developed and refined in efficiency to repair data damage and restore data to include updates from the last full database back up to the time of failure.

The Report Processing capabilities proved to be very popular in providing real-tme operation control and soon became essential information services.

Chapter 5

418 CRT-RPS – The Final Stages

By 1974, the system had been upgraded to larger 418 II and 418III processors.   Most of the factory operations departments had implemented reporting including Accounting, Quality Control, Systems Manufacturing and Engineering. Other Univac plants in Montreal, as well as Iowa and California were also connected in for Real-Time Report Processing services. Univac Marketing in

Chicago, IL., Minneapolis, MN. and King of Prussia, PA were also on-line. At its full implementation, the 418 CRT-RPS serviced more than 370 types of reporting with over 3,000 individual reports containing over 750,000 lines of data being maintained and processed.

All of this was accomplished without conventional programming of these interactive,real-tme report processing services. What was most important, the feasibility and popularity of Real-Tme Report Processing and programmerless user designed applications were clearly established. The system designers and supporters as well as corporate management were beginning to sense that Real-Time Report Processing concepts could have great potential.

The 418 CRT-RPS System, Full Implementation

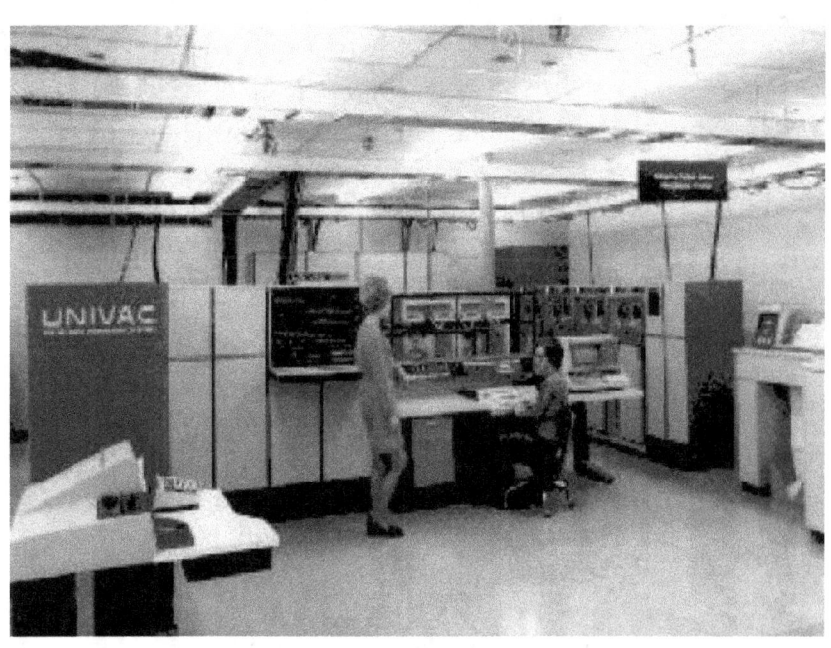

Chapter 6

418 CRT-RPS To RPS 1100 and MAPPER 1100
Beginning of the Main-Frame MAPPER 1100 System

The conversion of 418 CRT-RPS to the 1100 Main Frame systems required a new name for the project. A search for a new name was launched which ended with the name **MAPPER 1100** being chosen. The MAPPER acronym was defined as standing for Maintaining, Preparing and Producing Executive Reports. The idea of users being application designers suggested, jokingly, that MAPPER stood for; Make All Programming People Excessive & Redundant.

So the development of MAPPER 1100 proceeded. For maximum efficiency, MAPPER software was written in 1100 Assembler language.

During the design of the initial MAPPER 1100 system software, the existing functionality of 418 CRT-RPS was duplicated. This consisted of the following:

User Sign-on and off,
Mode (File Cabinet) Switching,
Form Generation (New Type of Reporting)
Report Index, Add, Delete, Duplicate, Display,
Line Roll, Add, Delete and Duplicate,
Search Single or Multiple Reports for single ID's,
Sort Reports or Results,
Find and Display (positional search),
Match data between reports,
Arithmetic and Totalize data analysis,
System High Speed and Remote Printing
Punch Card output,
Report Build Generation, RBG
Report Generation, RPG

New analytic functionality was added; multi-id search, fast access function call techniques, password security for data access, and

RPG (Report Generation) with Match capability and Station to Station (Email like) messaging.

The First MAPPER 1100 operations began in February of 1975 on an 1106 main-frame system.

By the end of 1975 over 250 terminals were configured for access to the IS&C MAPPER 1100 system. Most of the departments in the Roseville plant had user developed, operational, Real-Time Report Processing applications:

Production Control	Final Assembly,
Scheduling and Dispatching,	Shipping,
Quality and Reliability Control,	Site administration,
Final Test,	Transportation,
Purchasing,	DevelopmentCenter
Material Support,	Engineering, Drafting, etc.
Cost Accounting,	IS&C Project Status
Receiving,	

In addition to the Roseville plants, services were also provided to Sperry factory operations in:

Eagan MN,	Bristol TN,
Jackson MN,	Chicago IL,
MontrealCanada,	Elk Grove IL,
Utica NY,	Philadelphia PA,
Salt Lake City UT,	Cupertino CA.

Administrative reporting was also provided to departments in Univac Headquarters, Blue Bell PA.. Over 375 different types (applications) of reporting consisting of 1,500,000 lines of report data was available on line for real-time Report Processing.

Marketing offices did administrative reporting from:

Minneapolis MN,
Blue Bell PA,
Whitpain PA,
Toronto Canada,
Des Moines IA,
New York NY,
Dallas TX,
Montclair NJ,
Cleveland OH,
Kansas City
MO,

Phoenix AZ,
Washington DC,
Indianapolis IN,
Atlanta GA,
San Francisco CA,
Chicago IL,
Houston TX,
San Antonio TX,
Tulsa OK, etc.

This use of Real-Time Report Processing services by marketing for administrative purposes provided marketing exposure to these concepts which was instrumental in the development of the MAPPER 1100 market in the future.

Chapter 7

MAPPER 1100 Transition to Marketing

MAPPER 1100

CRT Report Processing System

UNISCOPE
Visual Communication Terminal

Since RPS 1100 was the official product version, MAPPER 1100 was not to be offered to Univac customers. It was only to be used internally in the corporation.

The Chicago salesman who finally broke the ice was Joseph (Joe) Bradway with the first sale of MAPPER 1100 to Santa Fe Railway.

Chapter 8

Santa Fe Railway, The First MAPPER 1100 Customer

This chapter includes the story of the use of MAPPER 1100 at Santa Fe Railway. It is truly remarkable and a great example of the potentials of user-designed applications as done with Real-Time Report Processing systems.

```
Santa Fe Railway's OX Project:
The World's Largest User-Developed Computer
System
```

The first commercial use of Sperry Univac's MAPPER 1100 was on the Santa Fe Railway in 1976. Since Santa Fe was the first and by far the largest of the MAPPER implementations, a spirit of cooperation developed that greatly accelerated the growth of MAPPER as an ultra-high-level language. Santa Fe got a great deal from this exchange as well.

According to James Martin, an internationally recognized expert and consultant on data processing, Santa Fe's OX (Operations Expeditor) project (the corporate name for the applications that used MAPPER) is **the world's largest user-developed computer system and a prime example of the path data processing will ultimately have to take worldwide. Today, the BIS Systems empower that user application development path.**

By 1982, over 2,500 terminals were on-line tracking over 68,000 cars in over 175 rail yards. The system used two Sperry 1100/84 central multi-processors and had a total value of over $25 Million. At that time Santa Fe also had a large complex of IBM type systems consisting of two IBM 3033's, an Amdahl V/62 and an Amdahl V/8 which were being used for conventional data processing by Santa Fe ISD.

Eventually Burlington Northern did successfully take over Santa Fe. These changes and the merger of Sperry and Burroughs to form Unisys created an environment that favored the large IBM data processing contingent at Santa Fe. These factors encouraged a final decree that MAPPER systems should be removed from Santa Fe data processing. This was accomplished by removing all MAPPER supporters and bringing in client server application alternatives. Needless to say, the transition was difficult and costly.

Chapter 9

More Early MAPPER 1100 Marketing

The Santa Fe sale was truly a breakthrough first sale. Joe Bradway, The Sperry Univac salesman for that account, was asked; how he could make such a sale when the head of Sperry Univac marketing had issued strict orders that the MAPPER 1100 system was not to be sold? Only the RPS 1100 product was to be presented as the Real-Time Report Processing software product. He said he knew they would not turn down such a large order.

GTE Automatic Electric

Shortly after the Santa Fe sale, another sale of MAPPER 1100 was made to GTE Automatic Electric. GTE had a critical problem in their Northlake plant trying to deal with their growing printed circuit manufacturing requirements using manual paper records. **Management required that a computerized shop floor control system be installed within 90 days.**

The GTE team examined 10 different systems from a variety of vendors. They were shown demonstrations of MAPPER 1100 and identified with the MAPPER users in the Sperry Univac Roseville plant who were running a similar printed circuit manufacturing operation using MAPPER applications that the users had developed. This real-time Report Processing was just what they needed. It was also critical that users could design the applications, programmers were not available from Data Processing in GTE.

The details of the GTE Automatic Electric MAPPER 1100 implementation along with personal opinions about this accomplishment are included in this chapter.

"At GTE, we did harness a **user-oriented report-processing system** to audit a system conversion and measure performance of both operations and the materials management function. Operations management must provide leadership. Data processing is too important to be left to the professionals. A Real-Time Report Processing system can get short-term results quickly and provide the basis for management change too dynamic for a structured system."

Chapter 10

MAPPER 1100 Expands and Gains Power

By 1978 other 1100 main frame computer system sales based on MAPPER 1100 were also made to FTD Florists and Sargent Lundy Engineering corporations and the Chicago Board of Education. Those sales were also made in the Chicago area.

The Sperry Univac branch in Kansas City saw the example of MAPPER 1100 as used in the Santa Fe computer center in Topeka, KS. This prompted another sale of MAPPER 1100 to Kansas City Power and Light.

All of the systems to that time had been sold as Category III products. This meant that standard company support would not be provided for such sales. **It is indicative of the appeal the MAPPER 1100 product had to these customers that they would purchase main frame computer systems with such a risky support policy.** The only support they could officially expect had to be provided by the local marketing branch.

These sales were lending credibility to the marketing potential of MAPPER 1100. However, the official company position was still that RPS 1100 was to be the only Real-Time Report Processing software product to be offered. One Sperry Univac marketing Vice President offered the "courageous" opinion that if seven main frame systems could be sold with MAPPER 1100 perhaps it could be given a standard Sperry Univac product designation.

Meanwhile the functionality (report processing capabilities) of MAPPER 1100 was constantly being enhanced. New releases of report processing functionality were being provided often more than once each year.

The view of the on-line report database was redefined to be more understandable by users. It was compared to a room full of "Electronic Filing Cabinets" easily understood by users.

MAPPER 1100 System

On–Line Data Base

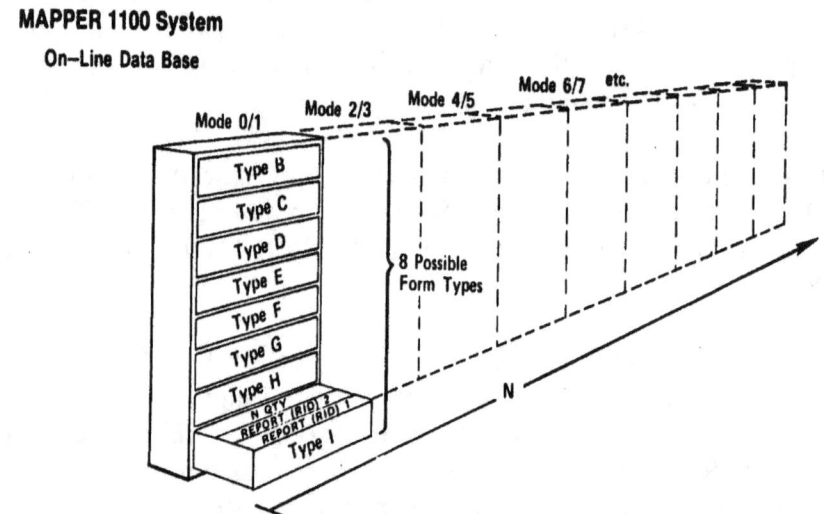

A large set of real-time, manually executed update, selection and computational analytic functions were provided:

A	Fortran-based equation calculator
ADON	Append a function Result or report to another report
AL	Alarm message reminder on a specified time and date.
AR	Add a report
AUX	Print reports on auxiliary printers
BATCHSTRT	Batch Processing start function
BATCHPORT	Batch processing port input
BF	Binary find process (Search and display to a data position)
CHG	Locate and change (update) a character string

COPY	Copy files from system to system
D	Display a report
DATE	Analyze dates within a report
DR	Delete a report
ELT	Copy a report to program file
F	Find characters in a report/reports
FORM	Form design and generation
I	Index a form Type (Drawer)
LINE-ADD,DEL	Line add, delete,
DUP,INS	Line duplicate, insert
LOC	Locate character string and display at that point in the report
MA	Match data in two reports
MAU	Match two reports and update
PR	Print a report or reports or result
PSW	Report update password
REP	Replace report with result/report
RET	Retrieve a file or element from other database outside of the RPS
RETR	Retrieve a report from history
RF	Reformat an existing report
RPSW	Report read access password
S	Search a report or reports in a type
SEND	Terminal to terminal report transmit
SORT	Sort a report or result
SS	Station to station message transfer
SU	Search report/s and update changes
TOT	Perform arithmetic on report data

MAPPER Real-Time Report Processing provides access from a distributed network of terminals to a commonly accessible report database. These reports could be displayed and updated within security limitations and, once updated; the changes could be seen immediately by anyone displaying the report, no SAVE required by users.

While real-time report data visibility and updating is extremely valuable, it is the processing of the reports using the manual functions to create Real Control Information where enormous productivity gains can be made.

These analytic functions process individual lines or reports or sets of reports within a Type of reports. When executed, these analytic functions produce full data sets called **Results**. This is different than a result produced by most PC information processors which usually only produce a screen of processed data at a time.

These Results could be further processed or refined using other functions. It is possible to process either Reports or Results with these functions. This is one of the characteristics that distinguishes MAPPER Real-Time Report Processing from typical PC information processing people see today.

Where repetitive patterns are encountered in the use of manual functions, RUN scripted procedures could be created that could execute the same function sequence with a single call.

EXAMPLE REPORT

```
.DATE    09 DEC 20   04:30:11   RID     2B   30 OCT 20   MAPCOORD
.Production Status Report           Corporate Production        B0002
*St.Status.By.Product    .Serial.Produc.Order.Cust.Produc.Produc.Ship
*CD. Date .IN. Type      .Number. Cost .Numbr.Code. Plan .Actual.Date
*==.======.==.==========.=======.======.=====.====.======.======.====
 IP 201224 LS BLACKBOX1 436767           20389 AMCO 201223 201224
 IP 201225 LS BLACKBOX1 436768           20390 AMCO 201223 201225
 IP 201219 LS BLACKBOX2 637071           20353 INTR 201218 201219
 OR 200110 LS BLACKBOX4                  94754 ARCO
 SC 200110 LS BLACKBOX5 675281           97441 FEDS 200131

                            .
                            .
                            .

 IP 201222 LS BLACKBOX5 737582           20040 AMCO 201222 201222
 SH 201222 LS BLACKBOX0 746327           54327 FEDS 201201 201202
 SH 201222 LS BLACKBOX6 368061           54438 FEDS 201201 201202
 SH 201209 LS BLACKBOX6 777324           54232 DICO 201207 201209
 SH 201203 LS BLACKBOX6 785367           52232 INTR 201207 201203
 IP 201216 LS BLACKBOX6 926581           89381 INTR 201215 201216
                ***** END REPORT *****
```

SEARCH REQUEST

When a request is made to process a report or set of reports, a Function Mask is displayed which consists of the headers from the report/s to be processed.

Parameter data is entered in the field/s to be processed below the headers. The Functions have options which can be entered in the line above the mask. The line Of *'s below the headers are used to control the processing of individual Character positions within the fields. The presence of an * means that character position will be processed. This is a search for shipped (SH) status.

```
              SEARCH REQUEST FUNCTION MASK
*St.Status.By. Product .Serial.Produc.Order.Cust.Produc.Produc.
*Cd. Date .In.  Type   .Number. Cost .Numbr.Code. Plan .Actual. Date .Order.Cod.
*==.======.==.=========.======.======.=====.====.======.======.======.====
 ** ****** ** ********* ****** ****** ********** ****** ****** ****** ***** ***
 SH
```

                    SEARCH RESULT PRODUCED
                           .
                 8 LINES FOUND, 42 SEARCHED
                           SH
                        . . .
```
            .DATE   04 SEP 20  10:17:30  RID    2B   30 OCT 20  MICRO
  .Production Status Report                   Corporate Production      B0002
  *St.Status.By. Product .Serial.Produc.Order.Cust.Produc.Produc. Ship .Ship .Spc.
  *Cd. Date .In.  Type   .Number. Cost .Numbr.Code. Plan .Actual. Cod.
  *==.======.==.=========.======.======.=====.====.======.======.
   SH 201203 LS BLACKBOX0 746327        54237 FEDS 201201 201202 201203 S8738
   SH 201202 LS BLACKBOX6 368061        54438 FEDS 201201 201201 201202 S6937
   SH 201209 LS BLACKBOX6 777324        54232 DICO 201207 201208 201209 S8538
   SH 201203 LS BLACKBOX6 785367        52203 ARCO 201201 201202 201203 S8934
   SH 201202 LS BLACKBOX7 744627        44232 INTR 201201 201201 201202 S8531
   SH 201203 LS BLACKBOX8 945327        74272 FEDS 201201 201202 201203 S8518
   SH 201204 LS BLACKBOX9 714577        64231 AMCO 201201 201203 201204 S8531
   SH 201206 LS GREENBOX7 669624        54682 AMCO 201201 201205 201206 S8553
                    ***** END REPORT *****
```

A key to the "user friendly" simplicity of the MAPPER language is the fact that <u>intuitively obvious function parameters are submitted in the context of the user's own data.</u> When they design the data form, they automatically create an application specific function control language.

        EXAMPLES OF SEARCH INPUT PARAMETERS AND OPTIONS

```
                H (Option,Delete search statistics)
*St.Status.By. Product .Serial.Produc.Order.Cust.Produc.Produc. Ship .Ship .Spc.
*Cd. Date .In.  Type   .Number. Cost .Numbr.Code. Plan .Actual. Date .Order.Cod.
*==.======.==.=========.======.======.=====.====.======.======.======.=====.===.
 ** ****** ** ********* ****** ****** ***** **** ****** ****** ****** ***** ***
 SH                     Single identifier

 SC                     Multiple
 SH                     identifiers

 SH          BLACKBOX/   AND condition with last character masked

             500000     Search in
 R           700000     Range
```

        Any number of fields can be searched at the same time.

EXAMPLES OF SORT INPUT PARAMETERS

```
*St.Status.By.  Produ  .Serial.Produc.Order.Cust.Produc.Produc.Spc.
*Cd. Date .In.  Type   .Number. Cost .Numbr.Code. Plan .Actual.Cod.
*==.======.==.=========.======.======.=====.====.======.======.====
** ****** ** ********* ****** ****** ***** **** ****** ****** ****
      1                          Single level sort, ascending order

      1D                         Single level sort, descending order

      1        2     Multiple level sort, both ascending

      1        2D    Multi-level, next ascending, 2nd descending
```

EXAMPLES OF TOTALIZER INPUT PARAMETERS

```
*Product   . Sub .Produc. Whole . Retail .Commiss.Space.
*Type      . Key .Cost  . Cost  . Sale$  .Charge .Req  .Quantity.
*=========.=====.======.=======.========.=======.=====.========.===
********* ***** ****** ******* ******** ******* ***** ******** **
Multiple vertical sums  +        +        +        +

Algebraic sums   +       -        +        -                 =

Horizontal multiply               *       =                  +
and vertical sum                          +

Adjust all       +10
                           Costs +10          =

Subtotals  S     +        + when Key changes

Averages         A    A       A        A

Subtotal   S     +                                  C
                           and grand
                           cumulate
```

Besides the users having the ability to selectively and manually execute Real-Time Report Processing functions, the RUN scripted language continued to develop into a powerful scripted application design language. The users could learn this RUN script language and build powerful applications. One of the reasons this language could be readily understood by users is the fact that much of it is derived directly from the steps of manual function execution.

For example, to execute a manual Search function, the report/s to be processed would be specified: (This would search all the reports in the B Drawer.)

SEARCH REPORT

Report or Drawer B_____
Format Number _____

The Function Mask would then be displayed:

```
*St.Status.By. Product .Serial.Produc.Order.Cust.Produc.Produc. Ship .Ship .Spc.
*Cd. Date .In. Type    .Number. Cost .Numbr.Code. Plan .Actual. Date .Order.Cod.
*==.======.==.=========.======.======.=====.====.======.======.=====.===.
** ****** ** ********* ****** ****** ***** **** ****** ****** ****** **** ***
SH
```

The equivalent RUN language script statement format for this process would be:

@SRH,B H 'STCD' *,SH .

```
                              |____ Data to be searched for.
                        |_____ Field to be searched.
                  |_____ H option
            |_____ All reports in B Drawer to be searched.
      |_____ Search command.
```

All the 150+ executable Real-Time Report Processing functions have equivalent RUN script statements. Thus, they all become powerful script statements in the RUN script language. When the users become experienced in using the manual functions and how they can be used in Real-Time Report Processing, they can be excellent RUN script designers because they know exactly how to use these analytic functions and what they can do.

In RUN script design, in addition to all the manual functions being usable, a full repertoire of RUN script statements for variable specification and control are also available as well full evaluation (IF,THEN) logic control. The ability to read and update individual lines of data with RUN control could be done. In the early stages, basic screen text formation and output could be done as well as screen input with variable data. In time, the RUN script language would become a truly complete, structured, application script language capable of the most modern designs and appearance.

Chapter 11

MAPPER 1100 Service Expansion

From the examples of Real-Time Report Processing done by the initial Test and Production Control departments, other users could see the benefits of Real-Time Report Processing. Most departments were frustrated with their ability to get their specialized information processing needs satisfied by conventional programming provided by the IS&C department.

So when they saw that they could develop their own applications with MAPPER Real-Time Report Processing their enthusiasm was immediate. After hour MAPPER Real-Time Report Processing training classes were set up by the Education department to educate new potential users.

The methods and results from these classes is discussed in this chapter.

The IS&C Western Utility Computing Center provided the primary MAPPER 1100 Report Processing services to Sperry Univac plants. By 1978 this MAPPER service had grown to a major information processing asset provided by IS&C Through out the corporation.

If professional IT organizations offer and support the very popular BIS User Designed Application Development and services, they will be greatly appreciated by the user community. Their technical support for the BIS system services will also significantly expand their computer system infrastructure as illustrated by the Sperry IS&C experience.

Main Frame Central Processor – U1100/81 with Magnetic Tape, Disc and Drum   storage and 2 High Speed Printers.

Over 480 Uniscope display terminals connected.

Factories & Departments Serviced:

Roseville, Plant 4, Building 1.

Mfg Production Control
Units and Systems Final Test
Industrial and Production Engineering
Factory Scheduling and Planning
Factory Quality
Preproduction Manufacturing
Purchasing
Site Administration
Diagnostic Programming
Factory Operations
Plant Engineering and Maintenance
Central MAPPER Coordination
Information Systems & Control (IS&C)

Roseville, Plant 2, Building 2.

Manufacturing Production Control
Midwest Region Computer Center
Support Engineering (field changes)
Technical Field Support
Material Support Liaison
Tear Down and Shipping

Roseville, Plant 3, Building 3.

Product Engineering
Project Planning and Reporting
Software Development and Support
General Services
Personnel
Marketing
Engineering Information Service Center
Publications and Specifications
Systems Support

Roseville, Plant 4, Building 4.

Manufacturing Production Control
Factory Quality
Receiving Stores and Crib
Finished Goods Inventory
Traffic and Shipping
Purchased Material Quality
Worldwide Semiconductor Facility
Returned Rental Equipment

Satellite Plants

Montreal Canada - Power Supply Manufacturing
Salt Lake City, Utah - Printed Circuit Facility
Jackson, Minnesota - Printed Circuit Manufacturing

Clear Lake, Iowa - Test and General Manufacturing

Dial-In Service, National

Corporate Administration, Philadelphia
Marketing Support, Philadelphia
Marketing Branches
Marketing Central Operations, Chicago
Product Development Liaison, Philadelphia
Customer Engineering, Philadelphia
Worldwide Marketing Development
Sperry Internal Auditing
IS&C Headquarters, Philadelphia
Asset Management, Philadelphia

MAPPER 1100 Real-Time Report Processing
Transactional Daily Activity

Over 170,000 total transactions
Over 40,000,000 lines of data processed
Over 20,000 updates (equivalent to 100,000
punched cards)
Over 10,000 searches of report/s
Over 30,000 Totalizations, Sorts,
RUN Script executions
Over 7,000 printouts and messages

MAPPER 1100 Real-Time Report Processing Database

Over 2,500,000 lines of report data on-line
Over 675 different kinds of user designed reporting applications
Over 10,000 individual reports
Extensive historical reports available

Other MRCC System Real-Time and Batch Processing

Real-time Transaction Processing System (TPS)
This is COBOL-DMS based. Over 40,000

transactions are done in this system along with
the MAPPER service.

MAPPER 1100 Batch Interface
With MAPPER Batch Start and Retrieve functions,
users can start batch RUNs with MAPPER data included.
They can also retrieve files from the batch
environment   into the MAPPER database.

**This MAPPER service with over 675 user-designed
applications was a major profitable asset to the users, IS&C
and the corporation. Marketing used it as a show case to
illustrate the reality and possibilities of Real-Time Report
Processing by bringing prospective customers in for plant
tours or to see demonstrations done in the marketing branches.
This accelerated the pressure to make MAPPER 1100 a
corporate supported product.**

From the beginning, the necessity and value of Real-Time Report
Processing services always had to be defended and specifically and
realistically justified because they were developed outside the
authorized IS&C DP services.

How these justifications were measured and successfully made is
detailed in this Chapter.

Chapter 12
MAPPER 1100 System– Coordination and Control

As the service grew, it became obvious that it was necessary to
manage system resources by monitoring database growth and Real-
Time Report Processing function use. **Users are restricted to
which Real-Time Report Processing functions and RUNs they
can use. Security control could be effectively tailored to each
individual user's and application needs.**

The Coordinator (Administrator) is provided tools that ensure
secure individual use and database efficiencies are available.
These are detailed in this chapter. **The ability to create a user**

safe, creative design environment was key to implementing user-designed computing and gain the full productivity benefits possible.

One of the most exciting aspects of watching proper, user-oriented, Real-Time Report Processing implementation in a user-community is to see the multifaceted ingenuity and innovative adaptation of computing power in the Real-Time Report Processing environment.

Ideal Coordination would create a Real-Time Report Processing environment where the users had an illusion of infinite capability.

Chapter 13
MAPPER Development & Evolution

This Chapter describes marketing expansion and full functional MAPPER development.   The characteristics of large-scale, real-time, user application design and implementation is also described.

By 1980 MAPPER 1100 sales had been made to Santa Fe Railroad, FTD Florists, Sargent Lundy Engineering and Kansas City Power and Light corporations and the Chicago Board of Education.

The reputation of MAPPER 1100 had also been recognized by international marketing, In 1981 it was authorized as a Category I, fully supported product available throughout the world.

The success of MAPPER with 1100 systems made it an obvious choice to be offered for use with UNIX systems.   This was called U Series MAPPER or MAPPER C software.

The evolution to other micro and midframe systems and international marketing and the creation of needed support services are detailed in this chapter.

MAPPER software is unique in the industry in this ability to do application migration across systems without application conversion. In 1992, UNIX MAPPER software was the first XOPEN application listed in the XOPEN registry.

X/Open Compliancy

- X/Open Registered Application
- Achieved certification on March 6, 1992
- Enrolled as the "first application" in the X/Open Application Registration directory

x/Open **X**
REGISTERED APPLICATION

Eventually over 500 main frame MAPPER 1100 systems were sold in *Japan.*

In 1985, a Chinese micro-MAPPER system was also created. With Sperry's help, a factory was set up in China to manufacture the Chinese micro-MAPPER systems. It had an enormous keyboard which represented a repertoire of Chinese language characters. This version of MAPPER Real-Time Report Processing had a limited success but it did indicate the universal appeal of this kind of information processing.

```
.DATE 01 APR 85  14:21:04  RID     14    26 MAR 85  HANS
              SYSTEM MESSAGES                                          G0074
H==========================================================================
```

星   PRESENTED TO

                        MR. H.A. TYABJI

      这是第一个中文 MAPPER 系统的示范   ON THE OCCASION
                                        OF THE FIRST DEMONSTRATION
                                        OF CHINESE LANGUAGE MAPPER

          一九八五年三月二十八日   28 MARCH 1985

N. Black   *Liu Hong Fa*   *(signature)*
N.A. BLACK   H.F. LIU   S. WONG
                          刘洪发

J. Eisner   *(signature)*   *(signature)*
J. EISNER   W.N. LIU   Z.Z. XU
                          刘卫民   徐志忠

(signature)   *W. Meinel*   *(signature)*
H. HERMANS   W. MEINEL   J-P. ZUNDEL

As the MAPPER market grew in the US and internationally, the users proved their creativity by providing a steady stream of analytic functional feature enhancement suggestions. New, major analytic functional releases were made almost annually. By the end of the Sperry Corporate era, a powerful array of Real-Time Report Processing functions, Information Power Tools, were created that is unique in the IT industry today.

MAPPER Real-Time Report Processing Information Power Tools; 150 analytic functions with 700+ options

Abort Process	Count Statistical Analysis
Acknowledge Message	Create File In 1100
Add Line/s	Create Help Result Extract
Add On Report/Result	Create Temporary Result Copy
Add Report	Create Temporary Data Format
Alpha to Octal Data Converter	Date & Time Computation
Append Data Line/s	Decode Encoded Report
Arithmetic (Formula Solution)	Delete Selected Data
Auxiliary Printers	Delete Line/s
Add new Report	Delete Report
Alpha to Octal Data Converter	Device Definition
Append Data Lines	Device Mapping
Arithmetic Algebraic Formula	Display Format
Solution	Display Graphics
Background RUN	Display Report
Batch Process Interface	Display/Hold Headings
Binary Find	DLC (Display Line Numbers)
Cabinet Switch	Drawer List (DL)
Calculate (Line By Line Logic)	Drawer Password
Calculate & Update Data	Drawer Table of Contents
Calendar Generation	Duplicate Line/s
Change Character String	Duplicate Report
Display Colors Control	Encode Report
Horizontal Character Count	Extract Data
Combine Report Data	Field Column Count
Communications Output	Find & Diplay At Location
Printer	Form Generation
Compare Report Data	Form Design

On-line User Help	Password Entry
Hold Characters On Screen	Print To System Printer
Hold Lines On Screen	Reform Form
Index Drawer	Reformat Report
Index User	Release Display
Insert Line/s	Remote System RUNs
Iterative Binary Find	Replace Report
Iterative Calculate	Report & Line Limits Display
Iterative Count	Report List
Iterative Date Analysis	Resume Process
Iterative Find	Retrieve System File
Iterative RUNs	Report Writer
Iterative Search	Save Report Version
Iterative Sort	Search Report/s
Iterative Totalize	Search Update Report/s
Language Switch	Send Report Station To Station
Line Control	(E-mail)
Line Data Statistics	Send Report to User (E-mail)
List Dictionary Data	On-line Coordinator Help
Locate & Display Character	Horizontal Shift Display
String	Sign Off
Locate Help Keywords	Sign On
Match Report Data	Sort Report
Match & Update Report Data	Sort & Replace Report
Move Data Line/s	Start System Program
Name Report	System Activity Display
Names List	Totalize Report Data
Octal to Alpha Data	Undo Previous Data Change
Conversion	UNIX Linux OS Interface
Repaint Screen	Update From Search/Match

These real-time Report Processing functions can be used by any user without programming. Each function can be turned on or off for each user if needed for security control. The users are limited only by their imagination, creative ability and system security policies. <u>An illusion of infinite capability can be created for users</u>.

With the availability of graphic and color display terminals and PCs graphic chart functions were created. These could create:

Bar Charts	Radar Charts
Block Charts	Scatter Charts
Line Charts	Target Charts
Mixed Bar and Text Charts	
Line Charts	Pareto Charts
3D Bar Charts	Time Line Charts
RADAR Chart	Scatter Chart
Multiple Chart	Organization Chart
Sign Maker	Graphics Scaler
Target Chart	Text Chart
Time Line Schedule Chart	

Users can choose from this rich array of functions to do their programmerless Real-Time Report Processing creating real operational control procedures. This is especially effective because the functions analyze Report data producing a Result set of data which can then be further refined by executing more functions including graphic or print processes.

Each user typically learns the analytic functions and options they use most. The primary functions of Search, Sort, Totalize and Match are very popular. These functions have equivalent functions that can do mass updates after the process is completed thereby providing great productivity in information update processing.

Iterative RUN utilities were provided to enable users to execute a function, save the completed function mask, alter the mask, and use it repetitively. The iterative RUN scripts created are:

IBINARY FIND   ICOUNT   IFIND   ISEARCH
ICALCULATE   IDATE   ISORT
ITOTALIZE

Two very powerful functions which have no equivalents in today's general purpose computer applications were provided at this time. One was the Count function and the other was the Calculate function.

The Count Function

The Count function is used to analyze and summarize data and statistics. Based on key fields, the Count function computes subtotals, percentages, averages, entry counts, and more.

The Calculate Function

The Calculate function is used to compute, compare, and replace numeric data, character strings, dates, and times in a Report. It has the ability to analyze Report data line by line and make logical decisions in the process.

The Calculate function is so functionally rich it is essentially an application development language in itself. One user was able to create a complete state and federal payroll process with this Calculate function alone. Another found it to be extremely valuable in the analysis and management of international monetary funds.

The **MAPPER RUN** script application development language also expanded in power and capability. All of the manual functions can be called with **RUN** script statements for execution in procedures. In addition to those functions, an extensive array of logic statements are also provided.

Additional RUN script Logic

Break Collected Data
Call Subroutine
Change Variable
Clear Abort Routine
Clear Error Routine
Clear Label Table
Clear Link To Other RUNs
Clear Subroutine
Close Window
Command Handler
Create Result Copy
Define Button
Define Constant
Define Edit Box
Define List Box
Define Menu Box
Define Text Box
Define Variable
Define Window
Exchange Variables
Execute Command
Exit Subroutine
Find and Read Line to Variable
Function Key
Function Key Input
Go To Statement
Hide Window
Other System Read Data
Other System RUNs
Other System Sign-off
Other System Sign-on
Other System Write Data

If Conditional
Hide Window
Input Variable
Insert Variable
Justify Variable
Language Select
Last Line Number
Link to Another RUN script
Load Field Name
Load Format Character
Load System Message
Load Variable
Load Variable Array
Local RUN Call
Network Off
Network Read
Network Remote
Network Return
Network RUNs
Network Sign-on
Network Write
Out Variable To Display
Output Mask
Peek Variables
Poke Variables
Pop Variables Stack
Push Variables Stack
Read Continuous Data lines
Read Line
Read Line Next
Read Password
Refresh Screen
Register Abort Routine

Reg. Error Routine
Aggregate Fetch
Aggregate Modify
Release Display
Remote RUN
Remove Variables
Rename Variables
Return Call Routine
Return Remote
Execute a RUN
RUN Status
RUN Subroutine

Schedule RUN script
Statements
Screen Control
Server Interface
Set Default Colors
Set Format Characters
Submit SQL Statement
Unlock Update Lock
Mass Update
Update Lock
Use Variable Name
Wait Delay
Write Line

Utilities were also provided to make RUN application design very efficient. RUN script statements can be generated from manual function execution with the Iterative utilities. Screen (menu) control logic can be generated with the SCGEN utility.

This makes it possible to present information <u>in any way</u> on the screen or in menus.

MAPPER systems are capable of supporting efficient, high volume real-time, random access, Real-Time Report Processing, along with large amounts of concurrent, real-time updating of the database.

These adjectives sound good but what do they really mean? What is considered efficient in a MAPPER system? How high is high volume? How real is real-time? What is the degree of randomness in access? What is the transaction mix in Real-Time Report Processing between manual functions and RUN executions? How much is real-time updating actually done in a significant MAPPER service? **To give these general terms some meaning statistics from a large-scale MAPPER service are detailed in this Chapter.**

It is estimated that this service provides annual savings of over $35 Million per year over alternate Reporting methods.

It gives strong testimony to the efficiency and potential of well promoted and Coordinated, user-designed, BIS/MAPPER Real-Time Report Processing system services.

The potential of MAPPER software functionality and RUN script design capability is to provide the most productive information processing and user application design environment in the computing industry.

The MAPPER RUN script language was so effective in rapid application development because RUN statements could call and execute the over 150 pre-programmed Real-Time Report Processing functions as part of their logic. Such analytic functions typically consisted of thousands of lines highly efficient assembler code which were pre-assembled. They automatically and efficiently perform major analytical processes such as search, sort, match, and calculate and resolve real-time database access and update conflicts.

Recovery, security and back-up procedures are also automatically provided and did not have to be programmed. Screen logic generators and dynamic debug tools accelerated development steps. The report structured MAPPER database also made database setup and design or modification easy and quick.

The macro analytic function logic, the logic generators and the automatic background support all have to be programmed uniquely for each application with other development languages. <u>With these advantages, MAPPER software can be very efficient in application development compared to conventional programming methods.</u>

The imagination and creativity of users as empowered with Real-Time Report Processing Information Power Tools and the RUN script language makes possible comprehensive, state-of-the-art application development by users or DP professionals.

RADS (Rapid Application Development Studio) system.

This is a toolset that magnifies the power of BIS by making it much faster and easier to create major business applications. It provides a structured development environment for use of BIS as a 4th Generation Language when designing comprehensive, major applications.

RADS is a complete Integrated Development Environment (IDE), with point-and-click wizards that eliminate the need for most low-level RUN script coding. As a result, BIS developers using RADS assemble, deliver and maintain major business solutions much more quickly and easily than ever before.

An early version of RADS was used to create PCME (Point & Click Environment), for selection of analytic function options which was integrated with BIS starting in 1999. The RADS toolset is itself a complex BIS application (written using BIS run script), a testimonial to the power and creative potential of BIS.

Chapter 14
MAPPER Systems Marketing Golden Age

By 1981, when MAPPER software products were authorized for world wide marketing, IS&C had these Mainframe MAPPER 1100 services in these Sperry plant locations:

Roseville MN. -   (2) 1108 and (1) 1100/80 systems
Blue Bell PA Headquarters -   (1) 1108 system
Bristol TN -   (1) 1100/20 system
Salt Lake City UT -   (1) 1108 system
San Jose CA -   (1) 1100/40 system
Frankfurt Germany -   (1) 1108 system

A detailed description of these services is provided in this Chapter as well as successful marketing methods and the resulting customer base.

 MAPPER Real-Time Report Processing by its general nature is applicable in all industries, government and organizations.

By 1983, it was stated that 80% of new Sperry customers were buying because of MAPPER software.

At the peak of the success of MAPPER marketing shortly after the merger of Sperry with Burroughs to form Unisys, the MAPPER system market looked like this:

MAPPER 1100 Systems 1,500   USA
MAPPER 1100 Systems 1,000 International
MAPPER 1100 Systems 500   Japan
MAPPER 5 Systems   600
Personal (PC)Mapper Systems   6,500
UNIX MAPPER Mid Frame Systems 4,300

The MAPPER World

Registered Terminals	935,000
Registered Users	1,031,000
RUN script Designers	77,000
Active Reporting Applications	1,169,000
Reports On-Line	71,500,000
Stored Lines of Data	14 Billion
Lines Processed Per Day	61 Billion
Transactions Per Day	2.7 Billion

Representative MAPPER Customers At That Time:
Manufacturing
Unisys, General Telephone & Electronics,
McDonnell Douglas, Nike
Transportation
Santa Fe RR., Northwest Airlines, America West
Airlines

Distribution
Subaru of America, King Bearing, Kesko
Retailing
Circle K, Floral Network
Banking
Union Bank of Switzerland, TS Bank
Insurance
Employers Mutual,
National Life, Kansas City Life
Construction
Bechtel Corp., Sargent & Lundy
Energy Production
Northern States Power,
Kansas City Power & Light
Recreation
Walt Disney Enterprises, Carnival Cruise Lines
Government
Many Federal, State and City Governments
DOD, State of Minnesota, Westchester County
NY, Hillsborough County FL, California and
NYC welfare systems.
Military Branches
US Army, Navy, Air force
The Air Force had the most MAPPER Systems
+ Many more

To be used by Government and Military customers, sophisticated security capabilities had to be provided such as: Data encription and dynamic password changing. This was in addition to the user function, station and data access limitations normally Provided.

The Subaru of America MAPPER 1100 Story is
also detailed in this Chapter

MAPPER Systems were translated for use into more than 15 foreign languages including Spanish, German, French even Chinese and Japanese.

At its peak under Sperry Corporation, MAPPER systems were installed world wide in a hardware base worth over $3 billion.

Chapter 15
MAPPER Systems and Unisys Corporation

This chapter details the merger of Burroughs and Sperry to form Unisys Corporation and the effects on MAPPER Systems, renamed BIS, Business Information Server. The nature of 4GL languages in comparison to MAPPER Systems is also defined as well as its use as the 1st Application Design Language for Users.

Considering the exceptional functional capabilities, ease-of-use, performance, networking, security, administrative controls, system auditing, recovery, etc., the MAPPER system is far superior to anything else – a giant step beyond any 4GL model of computer use. It supports the "1st Language" for user designed applications.

Chapter 16
Implementing Real-Time Report Processing Applications
For Greatest Potential

User designed, Real-time Report Processing applications have enormous productivity potential and are applicable in the operation of all businesses and institutions from the smallest to the largest.

It is possible for a small business to start such processing on a PC and then expand these applications and their related real-time data bases without reprogramming as they grow to any size system/s as the business requires. Such productivity and upward compatibility across systems create enormous tactical and competitive advantages only available In the BIS systems.

How to do this to achieve the greatest productivity benefits is defined in detail in this chapter.

A characteristic of the unstructured, user designed reporting application is that the up-to-date report "data" is turned into real, operational control information as transient demand occurs by the execution of the over 150 general-purpose, user executable Real-Time Report Processing functions such as Search, Sort, Match and Compute.

This is "Free Enterprise" computing of the highest order and utmost importance. It holds the greatest potential for broad-scale operational impact and productivity improvement in all businesses or institutions.

An evolutionary concept of real-time application user development is supportable. The ability to implement applications quickly, learn from the implementation, and quickly enhance the application is possible. The idea that this is programming in the usual sense is questioned in this chapter.

The Evolution of a Real-time Report Processing User to Application RUN Script Designer is described.

There is really no danger in allowing the users to become designers of RUN script applications. How A completely system-safe, controlled, user design environment can be created is described in this chapter.

Clearly, there is no danger in involving the innovative Power User members of the user-community in RUN script design. The real danger lies in not doing so. For then, that rich, innovative, productivity potential that exists in every user community is not realized.

Power User driven, real-time Report Processing services provide a powerful capability that enables a 1st generation of user designed application created productivity potential.

It is possible for a small business to start Real-Time Report Processing on a PC and then expand these applications and their related real-time data bases without reprogramming as they grow to any size system/s as the business requires. Such productivity and upward compatibility across systems create enormous tactical and competitive advantages.

Power User driven, real-time Report Processing services provide a powerful environment that enables user application design, a 1st generation of computer created productivity potential.

Chapter 17
Business Information Server, BIS (aka MAPPER)
A New Name & Image

Unisys MAPPER System Reduction and Neglect

This chapter discusses remaining internal BIS system uses and current Unisys BIS system marketing. It also defines Several ways in which the BIS systems opportunity can be exploited to increase the Unisys Corporation stock or spin off stock value.

Since1968, Added functional releases has been made almost every year since then, <u>hence its functional richness, which is unequaled in the industry.</u> <u>BIS is the World's most powerful productivity APP</u>

User designed, Real-time Report Processing applications have enormous productivity potential and are applicable in the operation of all businesses and institutions from the smallest to the largest. Such productivity and upward compatibility across systems provide enormous tactical and competitive advantages for Unisys and its BIS customers.

No other IT vendors offer in <u>one user executable, integrated, system scalable, high productivity real-time software system</u>:

Functionality available across a wide range of industry systems

An equivalent user-driven set of >150 Information
Power Tools with over 700 options
A Real-tme, User designed, Report Structured
Database with interfaces to industry standard
databases.
A complete, powerful 1st Application Design
Language for Users

Extensive screen, edit and application code generation
Client-Server Networking across a range of system
sizes and vendors
Internet Integration and accessibility
A full set of system, user and database security
controls

Upward application compatibility from MS Windows
PC's to mid-frame and main-frame industry systems.

BIS systems software has been constantly upgraded
to run on all of these state-of-the-art systems:

Unisys main frame OS 2200 ClearPath systems
Microsoft Windows Systems
LINUX Red Hat and SUSE Systems
SUN Solaris

Interfaces are available to create application that
integrate the BIS system capabilities and database
with industry relational database systems such as:

ORACLE, SYBASE, INFORMIX, MySQLServer
Object Database Connectivity (ODBC),
ADO.net; relational data access through Microsoft
NET Framework,
OLEDB; A Microsoft Object Linking and Embedding
Database
Messaging; Websphere MQ peer to peer Message
Queuing and Microsoft Messaging

Unisys has continued to invest in OS 2200 BIS Systems Development over the years and with increasing emphasis on improved performance in all system versions as well as BIS systems modernization. These modernization concepts encompass:

+ A modern Graphic User Interface (GUI Point & Click)   look and feel for control of the interactive Information Power Tools
+ A modern application development environment.
+GUI, Unified system and database administration   utilities.
+ Tools to aid in modernization of existing applications.
+ Expanding interoperability with industry software environments.
+ Improved Internet operability and integration
+Development of a tablet computer interface to BIS systems.

BIS systems have been Web enabled with the ICE Internet Commerce Enabler. BIS-ICE is a software integration solution that allows organizations to manage dynamic Internet Web services on a corporate Intranet or the public Internet and World Wide Web.

This chapter discusses the Unisys stock and marketing advantages and appeal of BIS systems. It is a best-kept IT secret.   It truly can be represented as a 1 st Application Design Language for USERS.

An important question is: "Why is the BIS/MAPPER system and story not aggressively marketed and unknown in the IT World though it was responsible for over $3 Billion of Sperry Corporation system sales in Manufacturing, Transportation, Distribution, Retailing, Banking, Insurance, Construction, Energy

Production, Recreation, Federal State and City Governments and all the Military Branches?

The author asked this question of his son who is a Senior Data Processing Analyst with Wells Fargo. He said, "Why would the Data Processing Establishments that provide System Analysts and Programmers requiring Computer Science Degrees to do application design services encourage the promotion of a system that suggests that end USERS can become effective designers of major system applications?"

If the potential of BIS product marketing is disregarded, it will be one of the greatest $$ opportunity misses in history. Properly executed it can be one of the greatest $$ successes!

Chapter 18

REAL-TIME REPORT PROCESSING
1st Real-Time Application Design Language for Users defined.

BIS Real-time Report Processing applications are upward compatible, meaning unlimited system scalability without conversion. Users can start with any size system and scale up to any size system without significant application conversions. This is unique in the industry and of major concern to company start ups or growing organizations and can represent enormous productivity savings as applications mature and must meet growth and change requirements.

REAL-TIME REPORT PROCESSING CONCEPTS

The BIS tool set is fully integrated for users sharing a common, real-time updated database. As events are reported, all on-line users can see them immediately (no user SAVEs). This provides a powerful alternative to the inadequacies of multiple, incompatible applications.

BIS systems with more than 150 Information Power Tools and over 700 options available in one system with user application development capability have unlimited productivity potential.

The database is presented to users as organized in easily understandable, reports in electronic file cabinets with complete access security control.

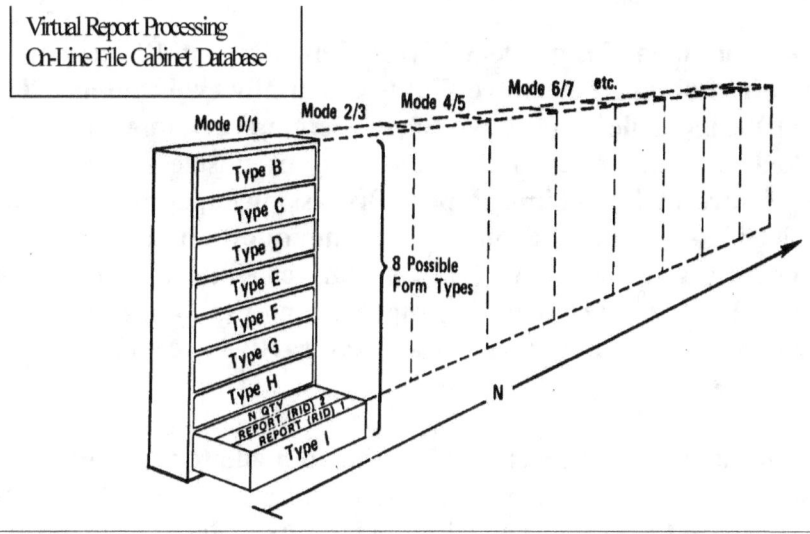

The user's data forms provide the means for Power Tool command control.

EXAMPLE: Function command parameters in an Automobile Inventory Database:

```
     ENTER options:          AUTOMOBILE INVENTORY
 *    Make      . Model .  Number .   Price .                  .
 *Automobile .           . License .Wholsale. Retail  . Schedl . 1 .
 *-----------.-------.---------.--------.---------.--------.----
 ********** ******* ******** ******** ********* ******* ***
  BUICK   <Search for a single identity
  BUICK        CENTURY <[AND condition, search for 2 identities]
                    MLS5933 <[OR  search for 2 identities
                    MKL4371 < in same field]
             5,000 <[Search in range, lower value
           R 15,000 <Search in range, upper value]
             +         + <[Verticalsummation/subtotal]
         [Days difference between dates]> +        -
             Sort in alphabetic order]> 1
```

Etc. Full logical computational capabilities are possible. Any number of fields or combinations of Parameters and options can be used. <u>The point is that data and intuitively obvious command parameters are submitted in the context of the user's own data. This is why users find these command procedures so easy to understand and use. Reports can be formed as above or they can contain textual or graphic information or any combination of these.</u>

The functional language of Real-Time Report Processing is used in a design procedure that is essentially evolutionary. The user-designer does not have to pre-define every question to be asked. As the questions occur, the user selects from the repertoire of Real-Time Report Processing functions the tools needed to derive the answer to the question at hand. By executing these analytic functions in real-time to accomplish the task, the user is actually programming the computer on the fly or in what is described as an "interactive execution mode" of analysis.

When they can define the logic paths immediately and evaluate each step as it is accomplished, making decisions based on results produced and choosing new paths of logic, causing the computer to follow the paths seen, is this not simply using computers? Why give it a scientific, professional mystique and call it "programming"?

The process of interactive problem solving is not a rigidly structured procedure. The minute-to-minute processing of real-control information is also not structured. It requires spontaneously devised logic derived on the basis of influences of the moment. Such procedures cannot be predefined.

Preparation of specifications in advance of such a problem solution is not only nonproductive but unnecessarily limiting. Once the analytic functions of computer command are so simple and natural that they can be defined and executed by the end-user, the pseudo-scientific aura that requires professional interpretation is gone. <u>So goes the Programmer, the Systems Analyst, the Systems Planner, and so goes the Specification Specialist relative to Real-Time Report application Processing</u> .

<u>The World's Greatest Productivity APP. THE Killer APP.</u>
<u>Real-Time Report Processing</u>

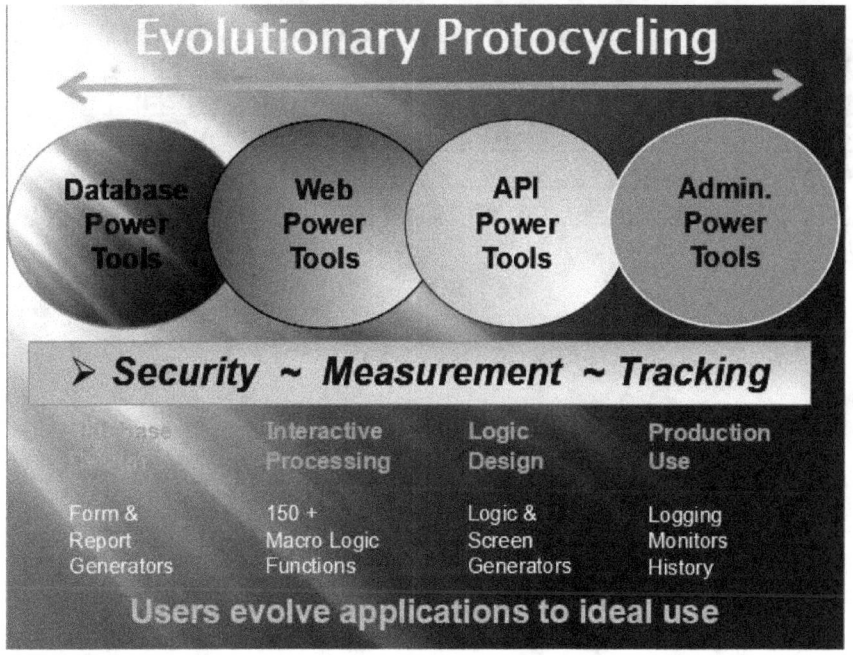

Applications can begin at any hardware level and evolve to meet all growth requirements with modern, "point & click" interfaces to over 150 interactive, Information Processing Power Tools with Over 700 options + real-time execution without programming, used on a shared, electronic filing cabinet report database, with full data base security, performance and application development and monitoring tools.

The universal potential for computer productivity with BIS Real-Time Report Processing is unlimited.

The fact that, originally, BIS/MAPPER systems required mid or main frame computing power for operation and can now operate on a laptop PC indicates how much conputing power is now available. Users, with their gifts of imagination and creativity, combined with BIS Real-Time Report Processing are users of the 1st Real-Time Application Design Language for Users.

Author Profile

Louis Schlueter is a data processing professional who is retired from Unisys after 34 years of service and experience in the industry. He held various technical, system test, engineering, manufacturing-planning as well as programming and management positions. He wrote the initial software design specification for Report Processing concepts on which the BIS/MAPPER system is based. He was also one of the initial programmers of the system.

He established the position and served as the MAPPER System Coordinator of the MSD MAPPER system in the Unisys Roseville, MN. plant. He was also instrumental in the development of the MAPPER system as a Unisys software product. He frequently consulted on the use of the system at Unisys user conferences, with Unisys marketing and at MAPPER system customer sites. He has written and had published numerous articles on MAPPER systems. He has also authored two books, "User-Designed Computing" and "User-Designed Computing, The Next Generation" in addition to this one.

Business Information Server, BIS
The World's Greatest
Productivity App.
CHAPTER INDEX: Key Point Summary

This summary document is not copyright protected and can be used for promotion of BIS/MAPPER. Search for this summary book on Amazon Books by Title, Author or:

Title ID: **6965374**
ISBN-13:
978-1544146348
ISBN-10:
1544146345

For The Complete 262 page Book:
Business Information Server, BIS
THE Killer App

Title ID: **5009830**
ISBN-13:
978-1502448583
ISBN-10:
1502448580

For an Introductory MAPPER/BIS Video:
https://youtu.be/g3BsxG8EvOo

Printed copies of the Summary and Book are also available from:Create Space Publishing:
https://www.createspace.com/

BIS Chapter Summary Site Link:
https://sites.google.com/site/businessinformationserverbis/

www.ingramcontent.com/pod-product-compliance
Lightning Source LLC
Chambersburg PA
CBHW071803200526
45167CB00017B/1300

* 9 7 8 1 5 4 4 1 4 6 3 4 8 *